THE LITTLE GUIDE TO

CHRISTIAN DIOR

Published in 2023 by OH!
An Imprint of Welbeck Non-Fiction Limited,
part of Welbeck Publishing Group.
Offices in: London – 20 Mortimer Street, London W1T 3JW
and Sydney – 205 Commonwealth Street, Surry Hills 2010
www.welbeckpublishing.com

Compilation text © Welbeck Non-Fiction Limited 2023
Design © Welbeck Non-Fiction Limited 2023

Disclaimer:

ISBN 978-1-80069-411-8

Compiled and written by: David Clayton
Editorial: Victoria Denne
Project manager: Russell Porter
Production: Jess Brisley

A CIP catalogue record for this book is available from the British Library

Printed in Dubai

10 9 8 7 6 5 4

THE LITTLE GUIDE TO

CHRISTIAN DIOR

STYLE TO LIVE BY

CONTENTS

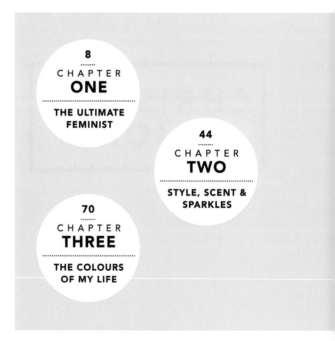

INTRODUCTION

Though his life was relatively short, Christian Ernest Dior's seismic influence on the fashion world ensures his name lives on as one of the most successful and celebrated designers of all time.

Using the rationing restrictions of wartime, he created designs that extenuated the female figure and released the women of the world from the restrictive, dull clothing that restricted rather than enhanced femininity.

After the Second World, it was Dior's sudden prominence on the world stage that restored Paris' reputation as the epicentre of the fashion world. To wear a Dior item of clothing was to wear the best of the best.

His post-war collection was described as a completely "new look" by the influential editor-in-chief of *Harper's Bazaar*, one of the world's most powerful style magazines.

The description was adopted and quickly became a fashion movement, with Dior's "New Look" leading the way and even stealing the limelight from compatriot Gabrielle "Coco" Chanel.

Yet his work was not without controversy, and his early collections earned him an equally powerful adversary in Chanel, who voiced publicly her dislike of Dior's fashion.

Despite Chanel's outspoken views on his work, each season, Dior's collection became the highlight of the fashion calendar as his global empire grew exponentially, making him a household name in a relatively short time.

Just two years before he died, Dior personally selected teenage assistant Yves Saint-Laurent to be his successor.

Though his untimely death at the age of 52 initially threw the fashion house into disarray, Dior – now driven by the precocious talents of protégé Saint-Laurent – recovered to maintain its status as one of the world's most luxurious and profitable brands.

Coming from a wealthy background with powerful allies, Christian Dior may not have had to scrap his way to the top as Coco Chanel did, but his talent is no less worthy and his legacy as one of the world's greatest designers is no less deserving.

CHAPTER
ONE

THE ULTIMATE FEMINIST

CHRISTIAN DIOR ADORED
WOMEN AND EVERYTHING THEY
REPRESENTED. HIS SOLE PURPOSE
IN LIFE WAS TO ACCENTUATE
A WOMAN'S BEAUTY WITH
CLOTHING, JEWELLERY, PERFUME
AND ACCESSORIES...

66

My dream? To make women happier and more beautiful.

99

Christian Dior's love of women was evident in everything he did, as seen on livinginfiftiesfashion.com, "Salute Mr Dior"

"

The world is wonderfully full of beautiful women whose shapes and tastes offer an inexhaustible diversity. My collection must cater individually for each one of them.

"

Dior's aim was to be as inclusive as possible, as cited in the New York Post, Raquel Laneri (2021)

"

Accept, accept! You must create the house of Christian Dior. Whatever the conditions, anything that they could offer you could not compare to the chance of today!

"

Madame Delahaye,

a trusted clairvoyant and confidante of Dior, responds to his news of an investor's offer and the question of what he should do

> **"**
>
> Women, with their sure instincts, realized that my intention was to make them not just more beautiful but also happier. **"**

As cited on Kidadl's "70 Best Christian Dior Quotes from the Famous Fashion Powerhouse"

Dior was born on
21 January 1905, in the
northern French seaside town
of Granville.

Christian was the second
of five children born to
Alexandre Louis Maurice Dior,
the owner of a highly successful
fertilizer manufacturer, and
his wife, Madeleine.

"

Women are most fascinating
between the ages of 35 and 40
after they have won a few races and
know how to pace themselves.

"

Dior believed life was a marathon, not a sprint –
as tweeted by @BritishVogue, 19 March 2014

66

My dream is to save women
from nature.

99

As seen on thecut.com, Veronique Hyland,
July 2014

66

Individuality will always be one of the conditions of real elegance.

99

Dior's unique outlook was to fight conformity, as seen on theglassmagazine.com, winter 2016

"

A woman's perfume tells more
about her than her handwriting.

"

Another pleasant truism from the great man –
as tweeted by @BritishVogue, 9 December 2013

Much of Christian Dior's very happy childhood was spent at the seaside residence Villa Les Rhumbs, near Granville in Normandy.

His mother Madeleine tended and created the home's spectacular garden, sparking her son's vivid imagination that would later inspire many of his future designs.

"

Don't buy much but make sure
that what you buy is good.

"

As seen in The Little Dictionary of Fashion: A Guide to
Dress Sense for Every Woman *by Christian Dior (2008)*

"

I adore you, but you dress women
like armchairs.

"

Coco Chanel's

outspoken view of Dior's game-changing "New Look"
range, as quoted in Harper's Bazaar *by Lauren Sanchez,*
3 September 2020

66

Midnight blue is the only colour that can ever compete with black.

99

As seen in Vine Magazine, *Issue 51, September 2011*

"

I wanted to be an architect…
Being a designer I have to
follow the laws, the principles
of architecture.

"

Christian Dior as quoted on The List.com's 'How Christian Dior Changed the World Fashion' by Reagan Kelly, December 2022

"

My brother loved designing costumes. I remember a Neptune costume he made for me, with a raffia skirt covered with shells, and another skirt painted with a Scottish motif.

"

Catherine Dior,

as cited in the New York Post, "Christian Dior's Sister was a WWII Hero", Raquel Laneri, October 2021

The pre-adolescent Dior loved storytelling and costumes.

His creations soon attracted the attention of his sister and cousins, who eagerly placed "orders" for his already outstanding designs for the Granville Carnival.

"

Dior Couture is like art – they are the art pieces of a fashion house. Each piece is unique and made by hand.

"

Patrick Demarchelier
(celebrated French fashion photographer)

praises Dior – as quoted on thegloss.com by Penny McCormick

"

You can never take too much care over the choice of your shoes.

"

Dior was not one for trainers – as cited on Town & Country's *"Famous Fashion Quotes", compiled by Sarah Lindig, 2014*

Dior's family moved to Paris when he was a young boy, and although he had a passion for art and architecture, his father pressured him to enrol at the École des Sciences Politiques, where he would study with the aim of one day becoming a diplomat.

❝

My mother, whom I adored, secretly wasted away and died of grief...; her death...marked me for life.

❞

As quoted in Christian Dior: The Man Who Made the World Look New *by Marie-France Pochna © V&A (1996)*

Dior's friend and neighbour – internationally known actress and singer Marlene Dietrich – attended his first fashion show in February 1947 and remained one of his biggest admirers during his lifetime.

66

Deep in every heart slumbers a dream, and the couturier knows it: every woman is a princess.

99

As seen on livinginfiftiesfashion.com, "Salute Mr Dior"

"

Dior makes me look good,
and I make Dior look good.

"

Barry Keoghan,

the Irish actor, as cited in the Irish Independent *by
Kirtsty Blake Knox, June 2017*

"

Women will be good for you and
bring about your success.

"

The words of a fortune-teller proved true for Dior
and his life work – as cited in Dior by Dior *© V&A (2008)*

"

The women who are loudest for short skirts will soon be wearing the longest dresses. I know very well the women.

"

As seen on theciteste.com's
"Best 40 Quotes by Christian Dior"

66

There is no such thing as an ugly woman – there are only the ones who do not know how to make themselves attractive.

99

As seen on theciteste.com's
"Best 40 Quotes by Christian Dior"

66

After women, flowers are the most lovely thing God has given the world.

99

A quote to cherish for all – as seen on
@Dior official Twitter feed, March 2014

After Dior graduated in 1928, his father allowed him to pursue his real passion – art.

With his father's financial backing, Dior opened a small art gallery – but his father stipulated the financial support was on the condition that the family name would not appear above the gallery door!

❝

Real woman should
be capricious.

❞

*As seen on theciteste.com's
"Best 40 Quotes by Christian Dior"*

"

He taught me the roots of my art.
I owe him a major part of my life,
and no matter what happened to
me later, I never forgot the years
I spent at his side.

"

Yves Saint-Laurent

*remembers his mentor Christian Dior, cited in
the Met catalogue, 1983*

In 1928, Christian's father's business collapsed in the Wall Street Crash and in 1931 he lost his beloved mother to septicaemia.

66

A dress is a piece of ephemeral architecture, designed to enhance the proportions of the female body.

99

As seen in The Little Dictionary of Fashion
by Christian Dior © V&A (2008)

"

You can instantly spot a Chanel woman, so I want to develop the Dior woman.

"

Raf Simons,

Belgian fashion designer, heir to the Dior throne 2012–15, as quoted in The Times, February 2014

66

I create so that each and every woman is the most beautiful.

99

As seen on livinginfiftiesfashion.com,
"Salute Mr Dior"

CHAPTER
TWO

STYLE, SCENT & SPARKLES

CHRISTIAN DIOR'S CREATIONS MAY NOT HAVE BEEN AFFORDABLE TO MANY, BUT HIS RANGE OF FASHION, ACCESSORIES AND PERFUME BECAME SOMETHING FOR MILLIONS OF WOMEN TO ASPIRE TO...

"

The less you can afford for your frocks, the more care you must take with your accessories.

"

As seen on livinginfiftiesfashion.com, "Salute Mr Dior"

"

Nothing is more elegant than a black skirt and sweater worn with a sparkling multi-stoned necklace.

"

Dior's simple vision for a classic look, seen in the Daily Telegraph's "Best Dior Quotes", 2011

Following the closing of his gallery, Dior began to make ends meet by selling his fashion sketches, and in 1935 he landed a job illustrating the magazine *Figaro Illustré*.

"

A country, a style or an epoch are interesting only for the idea behind them.

"

As cited in the New York Times Magazine, *"The Big Picture" by Alix Browne, December 2008*

66

The best clothes, the most wonderful jewels, the most glamorous beauty don't count without good grooming.

99

Dior believed all that glittered was not necessarily gold, as cited on Food For Thought, Grooming

"

Colour is what gives jewels
their worth. They light up
and enhance the face.

"

As quoted in the Daily Telegraph's *"Best Dior Quotes", 2011*

"

The detail is as important as the essential is. When it is inadequate, it destroys the whole outfit.

"

As seen on vogue.com's "6 Lessons to Learn from Dior"
by Peony Hirwani, January 2020

After two years' military service, in 1942 Dior began working for fashion designer Lucien Lelong. There, he and Pierre Balmain were the primary designers, and part of their remit was to dress the wives of Nazi officers and French collaborators.

Lelong saw this as a way of preserving the fashion industry throughout the conflict for both economic and artistic reasons.

66

It is not money that makes you well dressed: it is understanding.

99

As seen on @VogueFrance Twitter feed, September 2019

"

Make me a fragrance that
smells like love.

"

Dior's simple request (!) to his perfumers –
as cited on www.cafleurebon.com, February 2020

66

Perfume is the indispensable complement to the personality of women, the finishing touch on a dress.

99

As cited on LDN Diaries,
"So Dior" exhibition at Harrods, April 2013

> **"**
>
> Perfume is a note of woman's individuality. It is the last touch to her look. **"**

As cited on Kidadl's "75 Exciting Scent Quotes" compiled by Kidadl Team, July 2022

A great believer in omens and fate, Dior was about to meet an investor and renowned industrialist, Marcel Boussac, who wanted to hire him to reinvigorate the established

Philippe et Gaston fashion house by becoming Artistic Director. Just prior to the appointment, Dior trod on a star-shaped trinket outside the British Embassy. He interpreted this as a sign to move into business for himself. The investor he met instead decided to back Dior's vision…

> **The real proof of an elegant woman is what is on her feet.**

As cited in vogue.co.uk, April 2012

"

High heels? Painful pleasure.

"

As seen on livinginfiftiesfashion.com, "Salute Mr Dior"

"

Pumps go with everything.

"

As seen in The Little Dictionary of Fashion:
A Guide to Dress Sense for Every Woman
by Christian Dior © V&A (2008)

"

I think of my work as ephemeral architecture, dedicated to the beauty of the female body.

"

As seen on BBC.com's
"The formidable women behind the legendary Christian Dior"
by Lindsay Baker, 29 January 2019

Dior showed his debut collection on 12 February 1947, revealing no less than 90 different looks to the fashion world.

He named them Corolle and Huit, but influential American *Harper's Bazaar* editor Carmel Snow coined the phrase "New Look" for the collection and Dior's reputation was immediately set in stone as a designer of immense talent.

"

You want to reopen a house that was open before the war, but I don't think it's relevant today. It's 1946, the war is over, we have to appeal to people who are starting a new life after the war.

"

Christian Dior reveals his vision for post-war fashion, full of colour, style and vibrancy. As seen in Vanity Fair's "How Christian Dior Pioneered 75 Years of Feminist Fashion" by Leah Faye Cooper, July 2022

> **"**
> Long after one has forgotten what
> a woman has worn, the memory of
> her perfume lingers.
> **"**

Dior draws on his own experiences and memories,
as seen on livinginfiftiesfashion.com

In 1946, Dior launched his own house at 30 Avenue Montaigne in Paris – he employed three ateliers and a total staff of 85.

> "
>
> Haute couture is like an orchestra for which only Balenciaga is the conductor. The rest of us are just musicians, following the directions he gives us.
>
> "

As cited on the kunstmuseum.nl, "Balenciaga in Black",
September 2022

66

I wondered if I ought to transform myself in order to not disappoint my public. Perhaps I should go on a diet and renounce not only greed, but everything that made life worth living.

Dior was obsessed with trying to diet and improve his own look – as cited in Dior by Dior *© V&A (2008)*

While dresses, jewellery and perfume were all part of the rich tapestry Christian Dior created, he considered shoes to be vitally important in creating a stylish signature…

CHAPTER
THREE

THE COLOURS
OF MY LIFE

CHRISTIAN DIOR'S APPRECIATION
OF COLOURS AND THE MOOD AND
MESSAGES THEY CONVEY – OFTEN
INSPIRED BY THE FLORA AND
FAUNA OF HIS CHILDHOOD – IS
THE STUFF OF LEGEND...

66

I could write a book
about black.

99

*Dior did write a book about black – and many
other colours! As cited on bijouliving.com,
5 November 2010*

"

There is certainly a red
for everyone.

"

As cited in Hero Magazine *by Alex James Taylor's*
Carpe Diem Dior Homme FW16, January 2016

Dior's younger sister Catherine joined the French Resistance during the Second World War and was captured by the Gestapo. Though imprisoned at the Ravensbrück concentration camp, Catherine survived and was freed in 1945.

In 1947, Dior named his debut fragrance "Miss Dior" – a tribute to his beloved sister.

66

The tones of grey, pale turquoise and pink will prevail.

99

Dior was inspired by the gentle colours of his childhood home in Normandy – as cited on Vogue's "Inside Dior's New Home", May 2016

66

Black and white might be sufficient. But why deprive yourself of colour.

99

As seen on lucybertoldi.com, "Fashion Quotes to Live By"

"

You can wear black at any time.
You can wear it at any age. You may
wear it for almost any occasion; a
'little black frock' is essential to a
woman's wardrobe.

"

As seen on Gracious Quotes' "32 Christian Dior Quotes"

66

Black is the most slimming of all colours. It is the most flattering.

99

As cited on Quote Fancy's "Christian Dior Quotes"

Dior attracted some of the most talented assistants in Europe – one being Italian-born tailor Pierre Cardin, who was Dior's assistant in the late 1940s… before he left to open his own (ultimately) multi-million-dollar business.

"

Dior enjoys the trimmings of life. A bourgeois with his feet well planted in the soil of reality, he has remained as modest as a sugar violet in spite of eulogies that have been heaped upon him.

"

Cecil Beaton *(British photographer),*

as cited in Vogue, "How Christian Dior's Gardens Inspired Fashion Greatness" by Elizabeth Tyler, April 2020

> **"**
>
> When it comes to accessories, bright reds – scarlet, pillar-box red, crimson or cherry – are very cheerful and youthful.
>
> **"**

As cited in Hero Magazine *by Alex James Taylor's* Carpe Diem Dior Homme FW16, January 2016

A confirmed Anglophile, Dior's rapid rise in the fashion world resulted in an invite to stage a private presentation for the British royal family – although King George V reportedly forbade the young princesses, Elizabeth and Margaret, from wearing such lavish creations as Wartime Britain struggled on rationing.

"

I love grey.
It is the most practical and elegant
of the neutral colours.

As seen in The World According to Christian Dior *by*
Patrick Mauriès and Jean-Christophe Napias, February 2022

66

White is pure and simple and matches with everything.

99

As seen on TVRST.com's "54 White Color Quotes Inspiring Bright Pure Days and Reflection", April 2021

In 1951, Princess Margaret
was photographed by
Cecil Beaton wearing
a white silk organza
ballgown by Dior for her
21st birthday portrait.

"

A black dress is essential for every woman.

"

As seen on thefamouspeople.com

"

Every woman should have
something pink in her wardrobe.

"

As seen in La Réserve Mag, *"Christian Dior, Couture Colors"*
by Michèle Wouters

"

Zest is the secret of all beauty. There is no beauty that is attractive without zest.

"

As tweeted by Fashion Quotes *@DailyFashioQ,*
6 May 2017

66

Simplicity, good taste, and grooming are the three fundamentals of good dressing and these do not cost money.

99

As cited on Kidadl's "70 Best Christian Dior Quotes from the Famous Fashion Powerhouse" by Writvik Gupta, 13 January 2021

Having realized the importance of the "complete look", in 1949, Dior became the first couturier to arrange licensed production of his designs – despite fierce criticism from the haute couture brands, who saw mass reproduction as a cheapening of their bespoke industry.

>> They [dresses] are my daydreams, but they have passed from dreamland into the world of everyday items to wear. ''

As cited on Kidadl's "70 Best Christian Dior Quotes from the Famous Fashion Powerhouse" by Writvik Gupta, 13 January 2021

66

After all, flowers are the most lovely
thing God has given the world.

99

As cited in Town & Country Family Album
by Leena Kim, July 2013

66

I drew women-flowers, soft shoulders, fine waists like liana, and wide skirts like corolla.

As cited in Vogue, "How Christian Dior's Gardens Inspired Fashion Greatness" by Elizabeth Tyler, April 2020

In order to realize his dreams of giving every woman the chance to wear his creations, Dior allowed his designs to be manufactured globally.

Dresses, shoes, jewellery and perfume propelled the Dior brand to one of the most successful in the world. Other fashion houses soon followed Dior's business model.

66

You can never really go wrong if you take nature as an example.

99

As seen in The Little Dictionary of Fashion: A Guide to Dress Sense for Every Woman *by Christian Dior (2008)*

66

Fortunately, there are flowers.

99

Dior's love of flora and fauna was never far
from the surface – as cited on AnOther, article
by Jack Moss, July 2020

" This light genius, unique to our time and whose magic name includes God and gold.

Jean Cocteau,

French poet, playwright, novelist, designer, filmmaker, visual artist and critic, was a huge inspiration for Dior.

CHAPTER
FOUR

FASHIONISTA

CHRISTIAN DIOR QUICKLY
BECAME ONE OF FRANCE'S MOST
IMPORTANT FASHION DESIGNERS,
KNOWN FOR HIS UNIQUE
APPRECIATION OF THE FEMALE SEX
AND HIS ABILITY TO ENHANCE
THE BEAUTY OF EACH AND
EVERY WOMAN.

HIS EYE FOR DETAIL AND
CREATING MASTERPIECES MADE
HIM ONE OF THE WORLD'S MOST
IMPORTANT VOICES – WHEN DIOR
SPOKE, MILLIONS LISTENED...

66

Each of my collections contained a suit earmarked for success called Bobby.

99

Dior ensured his beloved dog Bobby played a role in his empire, as cited in Vogue, July 2020, written by Alice Newbold

66

The only queen I ever dressed was Eva Perón.

99

As cited on welum.com by Cinthia De Ciancia,
March 2018

In 1951 Dior bought the rambling Château de La Colle Noire in Montauroux, some 30 miles or so from Cannes.

He spent more and more time at his countryside retreat, taking great pleasure in restoring the sizeable gardens to remind him of his childhood home at Les Rhumbs.

He planted 150 almond trees and had an ornamental pool installed, similar to the pond he'd designed for his mother aged 15.

66

You must choose colours that match many things in your wardrobes.

99

As seen in The Little Dictionary of Fashion:
A Guide to Dress Sense for Every Woman
by Christian Dior © V&A (2008)

66

Without proper foundations, there can be no fashion.

99

*Dior's basic requirements of any project were
solid foundations – as cited on Quote Fancy's
"Christian Dior Quotes"*

"

In a machine age, dressmaking is one of the last refuges of the human, the personal, the inimitable.

"

As cited on the New York Times' *"On This Day"*
Christian Dior Obituary

"

I tried to show that fashion is an art. For that, I followed the counsel of my master Christian Dior and the imperishable lesson of Mademoiselle Chanel. I created for my era, and I tried to foresee what tomorrow would be.

"

Yves Saint-Laurent,

as cited on vogue.com (Australia), August 2013

"

In the world today, haute couture is one of the last repositories of the marvellous, and the couturiers the last possessors of the wand of Cinderella's Fairy Godmother.

"

As cited in the Strand Magazine *review of* Christian Dior: Designer of Dreams *by Aga Serdynska, 25 February 2019*

66

The American women will accept the new fashions.

99

As cited on Kidadl's "70 Best Christian Dior Quotes from the Famous Fashion Powerhouse" by Writvik Gupta, 13 January 2021

"

I think I would be more suited to the couture side of the business!

"

As cited on Kidadl's "70 Best Christian Dior Quotes from the Famous Fashion Powerhouse" by Writvik Gupta, 13 January 2021

❝

It was to be neither a château nor a weekend villa, but a real rural retreat, a part of the countryside, preferably with a stream running through it.

❞

Dior wrote his specifications for a new home after the success of his "New Look" collection – as cited in Architectural Digest, *Georgina Howell (2004)*

Dior's creations attracted the attention of Hollywood stars such as Rita Hayworth and Margot Fonteyn, who both bought and wore pieces.

Their endorsement helped raise the profile of the Dior House to previously unimaginable levels.

"

I wanted my first country home to look both lived in, and liveable in.

"

Dior wrote his specifications for a new home after the success of his "New Look" collection – as cited in Architectural Digest, *Georgina Howell (2004)*

LIFE magazine headline
THE HOUSE OF DIOR: NEW
FRENCH DESIGNER IS SURPRISE
SUCCESS AT FIRST SHOWING

"

God help the buyers who bought
before they saw this. It changes
everything.

"

LIFE Magazine, February 1947

66

No elegant woman follows
fashion slavishly.

99

As cited on Gracious Quotes'
"32 Best Christian Dior Quotes", November 2022

> **"**
>
> Even when there are no
> more secrets, fashion remains
> a mystery.
>
> **"**

As seen on livinginfiftiesfashion.com, "Salute Mr Dior"

Christian Dior transformed his country home of Le Moulin du Coudret from "a ruin in a swamp" by channelling the river, draining the marshes, and clearing the undergrowth.

He claimed the inspiration was from the peasant gardens which decorate the sides of the roads in his native Normandy.

"

From his very first works, it was clear that Henri Sauguet would bring spontaneity, romance, and a non-academic approach back to modern music.

"

Christian Dior's respect for French composer Sauguet is clear, as quoted in Christian Dior: The Man Who Made the World Look New *by Marie-France Pochna, 1996*

"

It can be said, without exaggeration, that, for us, our clients are our true collaborators.

"

As cited in The World According to Christian Dior
by Patrick Mauriès and Jean-Christophe Napias, February 2022

"

I wanted to be considered a good craftsman. I wanted my dresses to be constructed like buildings, moulded to the curves of the female form, stylizing its shape.

"

As cited on varisty.ca, "The ROM's Christian Dior exhibit is a must-see for fashion aficionados" by Isabel Armiento, 4 March 2018

66

My life and style owed almost everything to Les Rhumbs.

99

Dior drew many inspirations from his childhood
home, as cited in Vogue, "How Christian Dior's Gardens Inspired
Fashion Greatness" by Elizabeth Tyler, April 2020

Though Dior's favourite colour was red, throughout his lifetime he always had a love of grey and pink – colours that surrounded him as a child at Les Rhumbs – a plastered, rose villa in Granville, Normandy.

> **"**
>
> God, I love that dress. It makes me feel like a million dollars, but I just had so much fun. Men kept coming up to me all night and asking if they could water my flowers!
>
> **"**

Tina Turner

comments on the Dior dress she purchased for her 50th birthday

Dior's first British fashion show was held at London's Savoy Hotel in the Ballroom in 1950.

More than 4,000 fashionistas applied for just 500 tickets.

So successful was the show, the Queen Mother requested a private viewing the next morning for the rest of the royal family!

"

There is no other country in the world, besides my own, whose way of life I like so much.

"

Dior's love of the United Kingdom often shone through, as cited in Mail Online, Christian Dior: Designer of Dreams *review by Dianne Apen-Sadler, January 2019*

"

I love English traditions, English politeness, English architecture. I even love English cooking.

"

As cited in Mail Online, Christian Dior: Designer of Dreams *review by Dianne Apen-Sadler, January 2019*

"

He was a shy man. He generally entertained because he had to. He would call me in Paris and ask what I was doing that night. I would say, 'Nothing special. Will you have dinner with me?' and he would always say, 'Only if you're alone.

"

René Gruau, *fashion artist*, recalls a friendship with a very special, private man

Superstition played a huge role in Dior's life – something that intensified as he got older.

He would always name a coat in his new collection after his place of birth – Granville – and one of his models would wear a small bunch of his favourite flower, lily of the valley.

And no couture show began without a tarot card reading beforehand.

"

I think of this house now as my real home… the home where perhaps I will one day forget Christian Dior, Couturier, and become the neglected private individual again.

"

Dior, a confirmed homebird, in some ways yearned for a normal existence away from catwalks, critics and paparazzi – as seen on Architectural Digest, *Georgina Howell (2004)*

> **"**
>
> When Dior showed his epochal collection, Paris fashion had been cut off from the rest of the world during the German occupation. In places like New York and California in the United States designers were learning to develop their own style independent of the French leadership.
>
> **"**

Bernadine Morris,

renowned fashion critic for the NY Times (1981)

By the end of 1949, Dior accounted for 75% of France's fashion exports and 5% of France's exports as a whole.

"

Paris, on the other hand, represents the sense of finish and perfection. It is there, more than anywhere else, the quality of craftmanship is really understood and we Frenchmen must preserve his tradition.

"

Dior pays homage to the city he made his name in,
as cited in Dior by Dior *by Christian Dior © V&A (2008)*

"

Fashion has a life and laws of its own that are difficult for the ordinary intelligence to grasp.

"

As cited in Dior by Dior
by Christian Dior © V&A (2008)

Dior had a lifelong love of dogs, with cherished hound Bobby perhaps his best known four-legged friend.

Bobby even appeared on the J'appartiens à Miss Dior ("I belong to Miss Dior") perfume bottle in 1953!

CHAPTER
FIVE

ELEGANCE & BEAUTY

CHRISTIAN DIOR WAS OBSESSED
WITH ELEGANCE AND BEAUTY – IT
WAS THE DRIVING FORCE BEHIND
EVERYTHING HE CREATED AND
CENTRAL TO HIS WORK AND ALSO
HIS SIMPLISTIC OUTLOOK ON LIFE.

66

Happiness is the secret to all beauty; there is no beauty that is attractive without happiness.

99

As cited on Kidadl's "70 Best Christian Dior Quotes from the Famous Fashion Powerhouse" by Writvik Gupta, 13 January 2021

"

Changes just come about, and many things contribute when everybody is ready for them.

"

Christian Dior, as cited in the New York Times' *"On This Day" Christian Dior Obituary*

❝

Saint-Laurent is the only one worthy to carry on after me.

❞

As cited in the Irish Examiner, *"The Legendary Yves is Back in Fashion" by Louise O'Neill, 16 February 2014*

In 1955, Dior employed 19-year-old Yves Saint-Laurent as his design assistant. Two years later, Dior later met with Lucienne Mathieu-Saint-Laurent – Yves Saint-Laurent's mother – and told her that he had chosen her son to succeed him at Dior.

Lucienne admits she was puzzled by the statement, as Dior was only 50 at the time.

66

In an epoch as sombre as ours, luxury must be defended inch by inch.

As cited on New York Times' *"On This Day" Christian Dior Obituary*

99

"

No fashion is ever a success unless it is used as a form of seduction.

"

As cited on thefamouspeople.com

Dior slipped a dried sprig of lily of the valley into the hem of each and every one of his haute couture models, and always carried some with him in his pocket.

❝

Robert Piguet taught me the virtues of simplicity through which true elegance must come.

❞

Dior pays tribute to the Parisian fashion designer who taught him so much – as seen on Robert Piguet Parfums website

"

I have designed flower women.

"

Dior, commenting on the floral masterpieces
in his "New Look" range in 1947 – as cited on Parterre.com's
"On This Day"

Dior's creations were in demand for movie-makers, and he was nominated for the 1955 Academy Award for Best Costume Design for *Terminal Station*.

He was also nominated in 1967 for a BAFTA for Best British Costume for *Arabesque*.

66

Elegance must be the right combination of distinction, naturalness, care, and simplicity. Outside this, believe me, there is no elegance. Only pretension.

99

As seen on livinginfiftiesfashion.com, "Salute Mr Dior"

66

I try to speak about women now, and for the future. Dior has to be about female empowerment. Only with flowers? It's not enough.

99

Maria Grazia Chiuri,

creative director of Dior 2016–present, as interviewed by Lauren Indvik in Vogue, November 2017

> **❝**
> The bonds that join a designer
> and his clients are a reciprocal
> obligation; one could not exist
> without the other. **❞**

As seen in The World According to Christian Dior
by Patrick Mauriès and Jean-Christophe Napias, February 2022

"

Chance always comes to the aid of those who really want something.

"

A great believer in fate, Dior thought everything was pre-destined – as seen on dior.com, "The Story of Dior"

"

In Paris, couture is in the air.

"

As cited in The World According to Christian Dior
by Patrick Mauriès, Jean-Christophe Napias, February 2022

> **"**
>
> The Dior brand is so famous, everybody knows the name and they did even in his first ten years. I found this unbelievable book and realised that in 1954, after only seven years, he offered it in different languages with projects from scarves and socks to perfume.
>
> **"**

Maria Grazia, creative director of Dior, as quoted in British Vogue, July 2017

> **"**
>
> Dior is grateful that when fashion tires of him, he has been lucky and wise enough to save a nest egg on which to retire to his farm and cultivate his gardens.
>
> **"**

Cecil Beaton (British photographer),

as cited in Vogue, "How Christian Dior's Gardens Inspired Fashion Greatness" by Elizabeth Tyler, April 2020

66

If you have hooked legs, wear big decollete.

99

As cited on thefamouspeople.com

"

Christian Dior never wanted
to become Christian Dior.
He didn't mean to become
a household name.

"

Hélène Starkman, *Cultural Projects Manager
at Christian Dior Couture – as quoted in Vanity Fair's "How
Christian Dior Pioneered 75 Years of Feminist Fashion"
by Leah Faye Cooper, July 2022*

"

The dressing room is a picture of hell, whereas to the public it has to appear as a bouquet.

"

Christian Dior, as cited in the New York Times' *"On This Day" Christian Dior Obituary*

Notoriously superstitious, Dior's lucky number was eight – the original House of Dior was situated in the eighth district of Paris, had eight floors and eight workshops!

66

By being natural and sincere, one often can create revolutions without having sought them.

99

As cited on thefamouspeople.com

66

I want to escape. I am hoping for
a sudden catastrophe – even a
fatal one – that will prevent the
Collection from being shown.
I want to die.

99

*Dior famously started to feel unwell eight days before
a new collection was unveiled – the stress and anxiety
was something he never really conquered – as seen on*
Architectural Digest, *Georgina Howell (2004)*

66

The rich live the same all over the world.

99

As quoted in Christian Dior: The Man Who Made the World Look New *by Marie-France Pochna, 1996*

"

M. Dior, who remained a bachelor, once was described as 'diffident, unassuming, balding.' He was a hard worker, often insisted that his lunch – usually a salad, boiled ham and fruit – be taken to him in his studio, where the lights often stayed ablaze long into the night.

"

As seen in the New York Times, *"Christian Dior Obituary", 1957*

Before Dior's death in 1957, he arranged that his sister Catherine would take responsibility for his artistic heritage by becoming the moral heir to his estate.

Catherine took on the task with typical determination and studiousness, ensuring his couture creations, home and even his favourite playing cards were preserved and his autobiography remained in print.

"

It's putting femininity on a pedestal. To be proud of being a woman and being proud of every aspect of it. That is Dior.

"

Florence Muller,

historian and co-organizer of Christian Dior: Designer of Dreams, *at the Brooklyn Museum,* New York Post, *by Raquel Laneri, 2021*

"

It is astonishing how the passing
of one night permits one to isolate
that which one did not really like,
from that which one adores!

"

As seen in The Little Dictionary of Fashion
by Christian Dior, 2008

> **"**
>
> He made women feel special, loved – and not just through his clothes. At each of his salons, he had models of different skin tones and body types, so when a client visited, she could see the clothes on a woman who resembled her. He allowed you to visualize yourself in his clothes.
>
> **"**

Matthew Yokobosky *(Brooklyn Museum),*

as cited in the New York Post, *2021*

66

We went from losses to goods
seized by creditors, while
continuing to organize surrealist or
abstract exhibitions…

99

As quoted in Christian Dior: The Man Who Made the World
Look New *by Marie-France Pochna, 1996.*

CHAPTER
SIX

INFLUENCER & INFLUENCES

A GENIUS WHO CHANGED FASHION
FOREVER, CHRISTIAN DIOR MAY
HAVE ACCUMULATED INCREDIBLE
WEALTH IN A RELATIVELY SHORT
PERIOD OF TIME, BUT HE WAS
A PRIVATE MAN WHO ENJOYED
SIMPLE PLEASURES...

>

I'm a mild man, but I have violent tastes.

> As seen on Kidadl's "70 Best Christian Dior Quotes from the Famous Fashion Powerhouse" by Writvik Gupta, 13 January 2021

> "
> It appeared essential to me
> that [Christian Dior's] legacy be
> addressed with a new perspective:
> flowers and plants don't just serve
> an ornamental purpose, they
> are our environment. We have
> a commitment to care for them,
> today more than ever.
> "

Maria Grazia Chiuri,

*creative director of Dior 2016–present, as cited on
AnOther, article by Jack Moss, July 2020*

66

Every bite you eat stays in the mouth for two minutes, for two hours in stomach and for two months on hips.

99

As cited on Kidadl's "70 Best Christian Dior Quotes from the Famous Fashion Powerhouse" by Writvik Gupta, 13 January 2021

> **"**
>
> It is unforgivable to do what one doesn't love especially if one succeeds.
>
> **"**

As seen on theciteste.com's "Best 40 Quotes by Christian Dior"

On 24 October 1957,
Christian Dior died
after choking on a fishbone
and suffering a suspected
heart attack.

He had taken time out to try
to lose weight and was on
vacation in the Italian spa town
of Montecatini. He had been
playing cards just prior to his
death, aged only 52.

66

I always find the early years, when a man is carving out his career, the most exciting part of any autobiography. Unfortunately, once he has left these years behind and entered a more secure phase, all too often he can no longer understand and recreate the aspirations of the man he once was.

99

Dior believed the struggle was the real story –
as cited in Dior by Dior *by Christian Dior © V&A (2008)*

❝

If my poor mama had still been alive, I would never have tried.

❞

As quoted in Christian Dior: The Man Who Made the World Look New *by Marie-France Pochna, 1996*

> 66
>
> For me, working for Christian Dior was like a miracle had taken place. I had endless admiration for him. He was the most famous couturier of that time, and he was also capable of establishing a unique haute couture house and surrounding himself with irreplaceable people...
>
> 99

Yves Saint-Laurent,

as cited in the Met catalogue, 1983

Elizabeth Taylor wore the Soirée à Rio Dior dress when she accepted the Oscar for best actress in 1961 for her role in *Butterfield 8* – perhaps no coincidence that the number eight played a part...?

"

We were just a simple gathering of painters, writers, musicians and designers under the aegis of Jean Cocteau and Max Jacob.

"

Christian Dior as quoted in British Vogue on the friends who helped shape his ideas, Suzy Menkes July 2017

66

Raymonde was to become my second self. Or to be more accurate, my other half.

99

As quoted in Christian Dior's 1951 book Je Suis Couturier *–*
referring to Madame Raymonde Zehnacker,
the director of the design studio and inspiration to Dior

"

Raymonde is my exact complement: she plays reason to my fantasy, order to my imagination, discipline to my freedom, foresight to my recklessness, and she knows how to introduce peace into an atmosphere of strife.

"

As quoted in Christian Dior's 1951 book Je Suis Couturier – referring to Madame Raymonde Zehnacker, the director of the design studio and inspiration to Dior

Some 2,500 people attended his funeral, including all of his staff and famous clients led by the Duchess of Windsor.

Another 7,000 people stood outside the church as Paris came to a virtual standstill.

"

In short Raymonde has steered me successfully through the intricate world of fashion, in which I was still a novice in 1947.

"

As quoted in Christian Dior's 1951 book Je Suis Couturier *–*
referring to Madame Raymonde Zehnacker,
the director of the design studio and inspiration to Dior

66

Over the years she [Madame Raymonde] has become part of myself – of my dressmaking self, if I can so call it.

99

As quoted in Christian Dior's 1951 book Je Suis Couturier
– referring to Madame Raymonde Zehnacker,
the director of the design studio and inspiration to Dior

66

Madame Bricard is one of those people, increasingly rare, who make elegance their sole raison d'être. Gazing at life out of the windows of the Ritz, so to speak, she is superbly indifferent to such mundane concerns as politics, finance, or social change.

99

As quoted in Christian Dior's 1951 book Je Suis Couturier – referring to Mitzah Bricard, Dior's "technical genius" and head of millinery

66

Her moods, her extremes of behaviour, her faults, her entrances, her late appearances, her theatricality, her mode of speech, her unorthodox manner of dress, her jewels, in short her presence, bring the touch of absolute elegance so necessary to the fashion house.

99

As quoted in Christian Dior's 1951 book Je Suis Couturier – referring to Mitzah Bricard, often referred to as Christian Dior's muse

"

I knew that the presence [of Bricard] in my house would inspire me towards creation, as much as by her reactions – and even revolts – against my ideas, as by her agreements.

"

Dior on Mitzah Bricard, as quoted on BBC.com by Lindsay Baker, 2019

66

I like all the simple things of life,
such as small parties of old friends;
I detest the noise and bustle of the
world, and sudden, violent changes.

99

Dior preferred a humble life, away from the limelight –
as cited in Dior by Dior *by Christian Dior © V&A (2008)*

From Vietnam to Ireland, New York to Paris and Oslo to London, there are more than 500 Dior boutiques worldwide, including 75 in France, 110 in the USA and 10 in the UK.

Christian Dior is buried
at the Cimetière de Callian,
in Var, France.

At the time of his death,
Dior's house was earning more
than $20 million each year.

"

The most important feature
of my life – I would be both
ungrateful and untruthful if I failed
to acknowledge it immediately
– has been my good luck – and
I must acknowledge my debt
to the fortune tellers who have
predicted it.

"

*Humble as always, Dior believed luck played a
big part in his success – as cited in* Dior by Dior
by Christian Dior © V&A (2008)

66

All I required to be happy
was friendship and people
I could admire.

99

*As quoted in Harper's Bazaar, "6 things we learned
about Dior" by Julie Kosin, October 2015*

66

I am convinced my finest memories are yet to come, and even my past lies just behind me.

99

As cited in Dior by Dior *by Christian Dior © V&A (2008) – the words of a fortune-teller proved true for Dior and his life's work…*

Dior's legacy is a
multi-million-dollar business
that continues to go from
strength to strength.

A change in strategy saw
its profits go from $2.5 billion in
2017 to $6.6 billion in 2021.

Its strong growth
means it is close to overtaking
mega-brand rivals like
Gucci, Hermès – and Chanel.